Acknowledgements:

I would like to thank my family for always being supportive and encouraging. They make it all worthwhile. A special thank-you to my daughter-in-law, Elizabeth VanderPutten for editing this book. Her expertise is invaluable to me. I am grateful, especially, to Our Lady, who is my inspiration.

Disclaimer

Welcome to the Catholic Wife's Maglet! I hope you get much out of it.

Before you get started, I think it is important to clarify that if you have a husband who has an abuse problem (alcohol, gambling, pornography, drugs or physical abuse) then these principles do not necessarily apply and may even cause some harm.
So you need to decide, or get a good holy priest to help you decide, whether you need professional help.

BUT…if you are married to a regular, wonderful man who is part virtue, part fault….be they annoying, in-your-face type faults, then the principles laid out in these articles can apply to you.

I also realize that it is not all the wife's job to "fix" things. But when it comes right down to it, we can only change ourselves.

That is what this maglet focuses on…. changing ourselves.
And God will bless our efforts.

The Catholic Wife's Maglet

by Leane VanderPutten

A Catholic Wife's Prayer

O merciful Lord God, Who in the beginning didst take Eve out of the side of Adam and didst give her to him as a helpmate: grant me grace to live worthy of the honorable state of matrimony to which Thou hast called me, that I may love my husband with a pure and chaste love, acknowledging him as my head, and truly reverencing and obeying him in all good things; that thereby I may please him, and live with him in all Christian serenity.

Keep me from all worldliness and vanity. Help me, O Lord, that I may, under him, prudently and discreetly guide and govern his household.

Let no fault of mine aggravate any sins by which he may be especially tempted; enable me to soothe him in perplexity, to cheer him in difficulty, to refresh him in weariness, and, as far as may be, to advise him in doubt.

Give me understanding so to fulfill my part in the education of our children, that they may be our joy in this world and our glory in the next.

Grant that our perfect union here may be the beginning of the still more perfect and blissful union hereafter in Thy kingdom; and this I pray through Jesus Christ our Lord. Amen.

Copyright © 2018 Leane G. VanderPutten

All rights reserved.

ISBN
9781728759234

J.M.J.

+

Editor's Note

Dear Catholic Wives,
The following pages are for you...to inspire you in your daily walk as a godly, feminine, loving wife.
As wives, we have a unique calling, a calling that causes us to reach into our innermost being in order to give ourselves to our husbands the way Christ would desire.
As we learn in **Finer Femininity**, we, as women, have the awesome responsibility AND power to make or break our marriages and our relationships.
Let's not wait to fix it **after** it is broken.
The principles laid out in this maglet will work if we work them.
It is all about self-sacrifice, submission, thankfulness, kindness, graciousness, etc.
The world around us teaches the opposite and it is so easy for us to slip into this mindset.
Let us use Our Lady as our model and learn the virtues of **true womanhood.**
God bless you!
Leane VanderPutten

Table of Contents

A Grateful Heart..page 1

Seven Days of Prayer for Your Marriage................................page 2

Marriage and Sacrifice..page 4

Quotes...page 7

Who Is Right?..page 8

Being Selfish is Not OK..page 10

Showing Up for Life...page 12

The Wife, The Dispenser of Hospitality.................................page 15

Hectic Days for Helen..page 16

A Wise Woman's Economy..page 18

My Response is My Responsibility..page 20

What Does Acceptance Mean?...page 23

An Aura of Organization..page 24

Quotes..page 25

The Wife Desired is Patient..page 26

Our Thoughts, Our Destruction or Our Salvation..................page 30

Home Warming..page 32

Quotes..page 33

Unloving, Disrespectful...page 34

Financial Distress...page 36

9 Ways to Nurture Your Love..page 38

Always Choose Love..page 39

A Grateful Heart
by Leane VanderPutten, Painting by Arthur John Elsley

There is a method for post-Communion meditation that has helped me to stay focused after receiving Our Lord in the Eucharist. I think it was originally meant for children....but hey, we are all supposed to be as little children, aren't we?

It is easy and may help you, too. It is actually an acronym and some of you may use this method already. The acronym is FATHER and here is the method to use:

F – Acts of FAITH
A – Acts of ADORATION
T – Acts of THANKSGIVING
H – Acts of HUMILITY
E – ENTREATY
R – RESOLUTION

Easy enough to remember, right? And it fits right along with what we have learned about the four methods of prayer and the four ends of the sacrifice of the Mass – Adoration, Atonement, Thanksgiving, Petition....

When I get to the Thanksgiving part of this prayer, my heart overflows (when I am focused and not too distracted) with thankfulness for everything we have. It comes easily – to think of things I am grateful for.

It hasn't always come easy. But I have had to train myself to regularly look at the glass half-full instead of half-empty. I still get tripped up. But for the most part I am able to bring my mind back to what I have....which is so much.

There are so many suffering in this world of ours and when we are aware of this, it helps us to comprehend what we have. Although the news, etc. can bring us down, a proper dose (important – not too much!) of it makes us grateful. It gives us a reality check. And thankfulness SHOULD be our daily focus. Our Lord is very pleased with a thankful heart.

It may take a **gratitude journal** or just trying to remember to switch tracks on our train of thought if it begins to get negative and self-pitying. There is no room for that in a Catholic life. Let's "boot it out" of our lives! (Speaking to myself here, too, of course)! I'm not an expert at it, but getting better.....

There are many, many little things that happen in every day life that we can be thankful for. A good cup of tea or coffee? A homemade apple pie? A good movie? A stranger's smile? A friend who cares? In this time of disturbing world news, having a safe home, a haven to go home to, is something to be very thankful for. I'm grateful for the beautiful fall we have had. I grew up in Canada and at this time of year winter is getting its tight grip on each day.

We can also be thankful for the adversities in our lives because they have helped us to grow and to have compassion on others who are going through rough times.

Each day we need to practice having a thankful heart. All those little things I mentioned? Why not each day, be more aware of them and send a quick prayer of thanksgiving to God, who is the Author of all these things as we experience them throughout the day?

When you are having that tea and it warms you inside, thank God for it. When you are about to sit down with your family and play a board game and you realize what a gift your family is, thank God for it. When you get in that warm shower and the heat penetrates your sore body and gives it relief, thank God for it. When you lay your head down at night and it feels so good because you are so tired, thank God for it. What better way to train your mind to be thankful!

I read these words from a very wise woman: "Learn to enjoy life. Be thankful. Smile. When you catch yourself becoming irritated or disturbed at circumstances, stop and laugh at the little things that steal your peace. Count your blessings and learn to be appreciative."

Cicero once said, "A grateful heart is not only the greatest virtue, but the parent of all the other virtues."

So as each day passes, let us offer up our little inconveniences, our stresses, our fatigue for those less fortunate than ourselves. And, on the flip side, let's start becoming more aware of the little things and thanking God for them.

May Our Lord and Our Lady help us to become holy with hearts filled with love and gratefulness. Amen!

Seven Days of Prayer to Our Lady for Your Marriage

Monday:

Blessed Mother, help me to be a good wife today. Please help me to be kind, long-suffering and willing to bear all things. Please take my old habits, my erroneous ways of thinking and change them into patience, goodness, faithfulness, gentleness and self-control. Please help me to show my husband today that he is number one in my life, even if I do not feel it.

Tuesday:

Dear Blessed Mother, please help me to know myself, especially in regard to my husband. I pray that you will help me not to be unloving, critical, angry, resentful, disrespectful or unforgiving. Please help me to put all those aside and forgive him. Please help me to be an instrument of peace in our marriage today.

Wednesday:

Dear Blessed Mother, please help me to be my husband's helpmate and companion, his friend and his support. Please help me to make my home a beautiful place for him to come home to. I pray that I can take care of myself and stay attractive to him. Please help me to be a creative and confident woman, one that he can be proud to say is his wife.

Thursday:

Blessed Mother, please help me to not expect so much of my husband. Please help me to seek your Son to fulfill areas of my life where my husband cannot. Please help me to accept him today just as he is and love him for who he is.

Seven Days of Prayer to Our Lady for Your Marriage (continued)

Friday:

Dear Blessed Mother, today I would like to especially pray for my husband and all his needs, spiritual, physical, financial and emotional. You know what they are so I leave that in your hands. I pray that he will be open to receive our Lord's grace in order to be a strong and godly husband and father.

Saturday:

Blessed Mother, please help my husband and I to be a team and to work together. Please bring unity between us so that we can labor together in harmony. May we become like-minded in our faith, towards one another and in raising our children.

Sunday:

Blessed Mother, please help my husband and me to be more and more committed to you and to your Holy Catholic Church. Please help us to grow in faith and to pass that faith onto our children. May it permeate every aspect of our life so there is no question Who we put first in our lives so our children see this and learn from it. Thank you for our faith, may we never take it for granted.

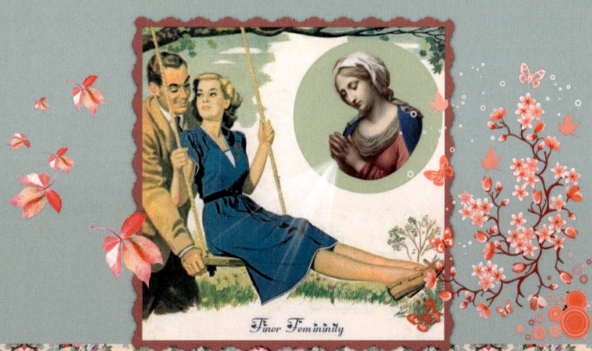

Marriage and Sacrifice
From Christ in the Home, 1950's by Fr. Raoul Plus, S.J.

It is not only the highest Catholic doctrine which requires the spirit of sacrifice of the married couple but more immediate common experience.

To live mutually in the closest proximity, in constant forgetfulness of self so that each of the two thinks only of the other requires something more than mere human attraction.

"Do not believe those who tell you that the road of love offers only the softest moss for your feet to tread. There are some sharp pebbles on the trail blazed by Adam and Eve."

The married woman who wrote those lines in verse, said the same thing in prose, a prose strangely poetic: "To enter into marriage with the idea that someday they will be rid of self is like putting a moth into a piece of wool. Whatever may be the embroidery, the gold threads, the rich colors, the piece of wool is destined to be eaten, chewed with holes and finally completely devoured.

It would be necessary for two saints to marry to be sure that no bitter word would ever be exchanged between them; even then it is not predictable what misunderstandings might crop up. Did not Saint Paul and Saint Barnabas have to separate because they had too many altercations? Then, can these two unfortunate children of Adam and Eve destined to struggle in life with all that life brings in our days of recurring difficulties expect never to have any temptations to wound each other and never to succumb to such provocations?"

If marriage is difficult even when the husband is a saint and the wife is a saint, how can we estimate the sacrifices it will require when the couple is, to put it briefly, but "poor, good Christians?"

Here however we are discussing the case of two who are sustained by dogma, morals, and the sacraments. But suppose one of the couple is a sort of pagan, or if baptized, so far removed from his baptism that nothing recalls any longer the mark of the children of God. What a secret cause for suffering!

Such was the suffering of Elizabeth Leseur who was happy in her married life in the sense that her husband was completely loyal to her but unhappy in her home because on the fundamental point for union, there was disunion, a separated life, the wife being Christian to the degree of astonishing intimacy with God and the husband remaining perfectly satisfied with the superficial life of so-called society.

Even when souls live in closest harmony, there will always be, even in the best of homes, a hidden cause for mutual suffering, which one author calls, "the eternal tragedy of the family, due to the fact that man and woman represent two distinct worlds whose limits never overlap."

For woman love is everything. For man it is but a part of life. The woman's whole life rotates about the interior of the home, unless necessity forces her to work to earn a livelihood.

The husband lives whole days much more outside the home than in it; he has his business, his office, his store, his shop, his factory.

Except for the early days of his married life, he is absorbed more by ambition than by love; in any case, his heart alone is not busy throughout his days, but also and frequently more often, his head.

Sometimes the wife suffers from not having her husband sufficiently to herself; the husband suffers because he appears not to be devoting himself sufficiently to his wife. Over and above other causes of tragedy, here is the eternal and hidden drama. Much virtue is needed by both to accept the suffering they unwittingly cause each other.

A MYSTIC MORAL BOND

Aside from the helps of Faith, two things especially can aid the married couple to practice mutual forbearance and to accept the sacrifices inherent in life together.

The first is the fact of their mutual share in the birth of their progeny.

Saint Augustine speaks beautifully of the two little arms of a child which draw the father and mother more closely together within the circle of their embrace as if to symbolize the living bond of union the child really is between them.

Even when one's choice of a marriage partner has been perfect, when ardent tenderness is evinced on both sides, there can still develop a period of tenseness and strained relations. Who can best reconcile the two souls momentarily at odds, upset for a time, or somewhat estranged? The child.

(Continued on following page)

Marriage and Sacrifice (con't)

Someone has said it well: "Life is long, an individual changes in the course of ten, fifteen, twenty years shared with another. If the couple has had a fall out, it will not be so perilous if they have known love in its fullness. I mean by that, the love of hearts and souls above all… if the two have the noble and deep memories which constitute our true nourishment during our voyage on earth, if they are above all bound together by the children that their love has brought into the world, then there is a good chance that even though they are caught by the undertow of passion, they will emerge safe and sound."

In addition to having children . . . that bond of love between the father and mother even in the greatest stress and strain . . . what most contributes to a speedy reconciliation after the clashes that eventually arise or the misunderstandings which set them at odds is the thought that they must endure, they must remain together.

What is to be thought of the following practice which is becoming quite customary? In the preparation of the trousseau, only the bride's initial is engraved on the silverware or embroidered on the linen. Does it not seem to be a provision for the possibility of a future separation?

By the constant repetition of the idea that man is fickle and that "her husband is the only man a woman can never get used to," the novel, the theater, the movies, set the stamp of approval on the "doctrine" of the broken marriage bond as something normal, something to be expected.

"On the contrary," says Henriette Charasson, who is a married woman and an author quoted before, "if husbands and wives realized that they were united for life, if they knew that nothing could permit them to establish another family elsewhere, how vigilant they would be not to let their precious and singular love be weakened; how they would seek, throughout their daily ups and downs, to keep vibrant, burning, and radiant, the love which binds them not only by the bond of their flesh but by the bond of their soul."

We must thank God if He has blessed our home by giving us many precious children; thank Him also for the Christian conviction which we received formerly in our homes, convictions which will never permit us to consider the possibility of the least fissure in our own family now.

A FATHER'S ANSWER TO HIS DAUGHTER

In the book "My Children and I" by Jerome K. Jerome, which is as full of humor as of common sense, a young girl tells her father that she is frightened at the possibility of love's brevity.

"Love," she says, "is only a stratagem of nature to have fun at our expense. He will tell me that I am everything to him. That will last six months, maybe a year if I am lucky, provided I don't come home with a red nose from walking in the wind; provided he doesn't catch me with my hair in curlers. It is not I whom he needs but what I represent to him of youth, novelty, mystery. And when he shall be satisfied in that? . . ."

Her father answers, "When the wonder and the poetry of desire shall be extinguished what will remain for you will be what already existed before the desire. If passion alone binds you, then God help you! If you have looked for pleasure only, Poor You!

But if behind the lover, there is a man (let us add a Christian); if behind this supposed goddess, sick with love, there is an upright and courageous woman (again let us add Christian); then, life is before you, not behind you. To live is to give not to receive.

Too few realize that it is the work which is the joy, not the pay; the game, not the points scored; the playing, not the gain. Fools marry, calculating the advantages they can draw from marriage, and that results in absolutely nothing. But the true rewards of marriage are called work, duty, responsibility. There are names more beautiful than goddess, angel, star, and queen; they are wife and mother.

(Continued on following page)

Marriage and Sacrifice (Conclusion)

MARRIAGE IS A SACRIFICE

In order to live these four last words, "Marriage is a sacrifice," it is not enough to have started off on a good footing, to be enthusiastic about fine ideals, to put all hope in mutual tenderness.

Since marriage calls for more than ordinary sacrifice, it will be necessary in order to remain faithful to the habit of sacrifice, to have more than ordinary helps.

We have already meditated on the similarity between the Eucharist and marriage; we have seen that not only is there a bond of resemblance between these two sacraments but that there is in the Eucharist, above all in participation in the Eucharistic sacrifice and in Holy Communion, a singular help for the married.

Prayer together must also be a help. Someone has rightly said, "The greatest sign of conjugal love is not given by encircling arms in an embrace but by bended knees in common prayer."

In his "Confessions," Saint Augustine describes his last evening with his mother at Ostia. It is worth quoting. When a husband and wife have reached such a degree of soul-union in God, they can face all life's tempests without trembling.

"Forgetting the past and looking toward the future, we pondered together in Your Presence, O my God, the living Truth, on what the eternal life of the elect would be like.... We came to this conclusion: The sensible pleasures of the flesh in their intensest degree and in all the attractiveness that material things can have, offer nothing that can compare with the sweetness of the life beyond, nor do they even deserve mention. In a transport of love, we tried to lift ourselves to You there...."

I must understand more clearly than in the past how essential it is to be rooted in prayer and if possible in prayer together.

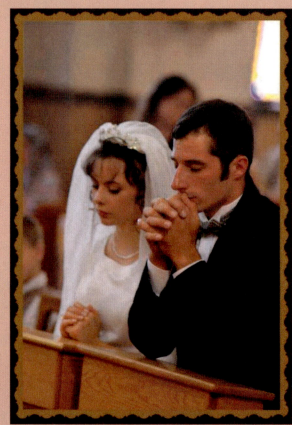

"How beautiful it would be if, during their evening prayer together, there could be a pause such as the one for the examination of conscience during which time a husband and wife would pray silently for the other, recommending to God all the other's intentions sensed, guessed, and known as well as those that only God, the Master of consciences, could know. Even more beautiful would it be if they would receive Holy Communion together frequently so that each of them could speak more intimately to Our Lord about the needs of the other, begging not only temporal but spiritual favors for this cherished soul."

– Fr. Raoul Plus, S.J., Christ in the Home

Quotes

No one can arrive at happiness through oneself, through self-seeking. If the wife has as her object the comfort and the contentment of her husband, she need not fear for herself. Only those who seek themselves need fear for themselves.
— Fr. Leo Kinsella, The Wife Desired

No woman will attain the goal of success and happiness as a desirable wife, unless her efforts are supplemented with God's help. She who builds without God builds in vain.
— Fr. Raoul Plus, S.J.

The happy wife brings happiness to her husband. He loves to be in her presence because he is happy there.
— Fr. Leo Kinsella, The Wife Desired

Don't compare your love story to those you watch in movies. They're written by scriptwriters, yours is written by God.
— Unknown

Remember it is not by push or persuasion that you bring out the best in your husband and impel him to a more successful and righteous life, but by an unwavering belief in his better side.
— Fascinating Womanhood

"Submission doesn't mean that we're weak-minded, feeble, or frail. It means that we're empowered by choice, and that we're dedicated to esteeming others higher than ourselves."
— Darlene Schacht

Who Is Right?
by Leane VanderPutten

"Why hasn't anyone told me this before?"
That is exactly what one woman said at our last Finer Femininity meeting. Our meeting was on the subject of "Who IS right?" when it comes to marital conflict.
It was very enlightening and I wish to pass some of it along to you.
Mr. Eggerichs (from Love and Respect Ministries) explains that when faced with conflict with our spouse, one person is not right and the other person wrong. No, we are just different.
We have different tastes, different preferences, different backgrounds…..we see things from different perspectives. Makes sense, right?
So why do we try so hard to prove we are right when in conflict? We are not talking moral issues here, we are talking about the day in, day out conflicts we have with living so closely, so intimately with someone…..our spouse. He gives the example of a husband and wife discussing the decorating of the interior of the home. The man wants a big overstuffed, leather couch and a display of all his hunting trophies hung in the living room. The woman wants the floral, Victorian couch and loveseat and would prefer not having the trophies in the living room, wanting to decorate with silk, flower wreaths and candles. Who is right? Well…neither one is wrong. They just see things through different eyes.
Many of the conflicts we run into each day are just a matter of perspective. Knowing this, we can try to stand back and see his point of view. That doesn't mean we have to always squelch our own desires, but we need to ask ourselves how important it is for us to push our viewpoint. Sometimes it may be important enough, often it is not.
Mr. Eggerichs also said that when a man and woman are in conflict, the man tends to stonewall (shut down) and the woman tends to move toward the man, wanting to communicate and work it out (oftentimes sounding disrespectful).
We tend to see his reaction of shutting down (I don't want to talk about it, just drop it) as very unloving. But, and this is the part that was very interesting to learn, research has shown that when a man is in conflict and his heart rate gets to ninety-nine beats per minute or above, he goes into "fight or flight" mode. Instinctively he knows he needs to back off or he'll attack.
So, ladies, when your husband shuts down and doesn't want to talk about it, he is actually doing the chivalrous thing. He does not want to fight, so he walks away from it.
"Further research at the University of Washington also revealed that of those who stonewall or pull back during marital conflict, 85% are men, whereas only 15% are women. In other words, women generally move forward to talk so they can resolve the problem. And while you don't mean to be critical, you can come across that way at times. This criticism is interpreted by your husbands as disrespect, which escalates the conflict for him. Most men will then pull back because they believe it is the honorable thing to do. They know that if they don't withdraw, they will likely escalate the conflict and may possibly get out of control. This withdrawal feels unloving to his wife who is more verbal and is moving towards him to connect and resolve the conflict. So, although he pulls back to protect her, she labels him as unloving. No wonder things get crazy!" – Emmerson Eggerichs
This is important to remember next time a conflict comes up. A husband's deepest felt need is for respect. During conflict, he needs to feel his wife's respect. We need to watch our tone, looks, words and actions, that they do not come off as disrespectful, even if we are feeling it.
We will turn to Our Lady and ask her, next time we get upset about something, to first decide if it is important enough to bring up to our husbands. If it is, let us ask for the grace to talk about it at the right time (not when we are tired and cranky), and then, not to come across as disrespectful.
(Continued on the following page….)

Who Is Right? (Con't)

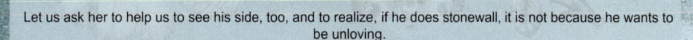

Let us ask her to help us to see his side, too, and to realize, if he does stonewall, it is not because he wants to be unloving.

"This week if there is a conflict, we want you to remain verbally quiet, when you want to argue or defend yourself. We are not kidding. See if you can go quiet and remain quiet. Remember, you are slowing down the Crazy Cycle by doing this. You can do it!"

Does this take work? Is it hard? Is it worth it? Yes, yes and yes!

Remember this: Our Lord never said it was going to be easy. But He did say He is with us every step of the way. Our marriage is the most valuable thing we have on this earth, besides our Faith. So it is worth the struggle to overcome ourselves on a daily basis.

We don't have to be a doormat....no. We need to be strong and dignified, but we must also give until it hurts. Wives and mothers know this, we experience it regularly.

The men have their own work to do in the relationship but we pray and leave that part up to God. We can only change ourselves.

We will turn to Our Lady and ask her to help us to have a quiet spirit, that we do not return what we deem as unloving actions or words with disrespect, but that we remain quiet. And that it is a **good** quiet, not one with a bad attitude.

Our Lady, Seat of Wisdom, pray for us!

In spite of all its trials, marriage promises to the young couple happiness in abundance. There is the first happiness of home-making and the supreme joy that comes when they look upon their first-born and know it to be theirs. Strength comes of working out together life's problems and of "having sorrow and doubling joy by sharing them." Pride thrills them as their sons grow strong and their daughters charming. Courage springs from knowing that they do not work nor walk alone. Then, when their work is largely done and their children go off to found their own families or give themselves to God, they feel the calm happiness of turning their faces toward heaven with the sense of a gathered harvest, full granaries, and their Master waiting to bless them for a crowded and useful life. –Fr. Daniel A. Lord

The understanding, the sympathy, and the patience required for happy living cannot be measured out.
The expression "marriage is a fifty-fifty deal" implies yardsticks, tape measures, half-cups, full tablespoons, and the like.
Love has nothing to do with these things--will not be fenced in by them, for love partakes of the very limitlessness of God.
-Fr. Leo Kinsella

Remember, we can't change him, we must accept and respect him. We should recall the things we loved about him when we first knew him.
Let's sit down and write those things out. We will make the effort, even if it doesn't seem like it will help. God is not outdone in generostiy! He WILL meet us more than halfway!
Let's not give up seeking for ways to make our relationship better. It is what we are called to do. Yes, I know the struggles are real. The solutions are, too, if we keep looking and striving. It may not be overnight, but, in time, you will see that your perseverance has paid off. - Leane VanderPutten

Finer Femininity

This is part of the deep drama of marriage: the constant call to "die to yourself" for the sake of your loved one.
- Alice von Hildebrand

Being Selfish is Not OK

**From The Good Wife's Guide: Embracing Your Role as a Helpmeet
by Darlene Schacht**

While switching channels one day, I happened upon an interview. Since they were talking about family, it caught my attention so I paused to listen.

"Family... children..." I heard those words. Could she have the same passion and convictions as I? I turned up the volume anxious to hear more.

Unfortunately what I heard didn't resemble Christian living by any stretch of the imagination. In fact it was so absurd that I turned the television off and considered cutting cable altogether.

My stomach was in knots over the attitude of acceptance that prevailed in this interview and the fact that they let this guest have air time.

After working overseas for a few months, this woman simply decided that she didn't want to be a mother any longer. She walked away from her two children (ages 3 and 5) and her husband of 20 years to build a career.

While away, she missed her kids, but she "didn't miss when they were throwing up seven times during the middle of the night, and getting a call asking, 'Can you wash pillows?'"

What has this world come to when children are discarded like items on a yard sale table? When we say, "I don't want to handle the responsibility that comes with being a parent, so I'll step away—while someone else carries my load."

It's one thing to buy a pair of boots and change your mind a month or two down the road; it's an entirely different thing to walk away from responsibility because life isn't what we hoped it would be.

"Everybody has their own choices," she said, "but my choice works for us and I think it's not so selfish for women to say 'Okay, I would like to have my own priority, I would like to have something in my life. I would like to be able to do my job.'"

"Not so selfish?" Is she serious?

That statement is the very definition of the word selfish: Devoted to or caring only for oneself; concerned primarily with one's own interest, benefits, welfare, etc., regardless of others. (Dictionary.com)

As wives and mothers we can and should have our own interests, but when our primary concern is our "self" to the point that we become our first priority, we have given in to a selfish nature that isn't lined up with scripture.

Unselfish Love

Everyone has the right to make their own choices—we do, but when those choices affect the welfare of children, we as a society should be moral enough to stand up against these ideas and teach women that being selfish is not "okay."

Titus 2 exhorts women to love their children and to be keepers of the home. That doesn't mean that we can't have our own interests or earn extra money, but it does mean that we are to prioritize family because that's what love does.

Love is not self-seeking. When you truly love someone you get up in the middle of the night to wash pillows, regardless of how much those sheets stink, or how tired you are.

Being Selfish is Not OK (con't)

The Problem – Or Is It?

In 1963, Betty Friedan published a book called The Feminine Mystique. For only .75 cents a copy, women would find the answers to "the problem that has no name." This book was the catalyst for the second–and what appears to be the most damaging–wave of women's liberation.

"The problem is always being the children's mommy, or the minister's wife and never being myself."
- Feminine Mystique, Chapter 1.

Apparently there was a "problem" that was plaguing housewives of the day, and according to the author, this problem could be fixed. If women turned inward and began to focus on their needs, their careers, and their happiness, they would find the happiness and sexual fulfillment they had been missing out on all along.

Since the author wasn't able to give "the problem" a name–let me. It's called, "sacrificial love," and according to the Bible, it's the only love worth giving.

Love is patient, love is kind. It does not envy, it does not boast, it is not proud. It does not dishonor others, it is not self-seeking, it is not easily angered, it keeps no record of wrongs.

Love does not delight in evil but rejoices with the truth. It always protects, always trusts, always hopes, always perseveres. Was there really a "problem" or were a few women creating an issue that didn't exist?

I pray that women today will step up and realize the fallacy that this teaching offers. Seeking fulfillment by putting our own needs ahead of others brings temporal highs that fade quickly.

If you're seeking true joy with long-lasting results, it can only be found by building virtue upon faith. That's where you'll find fulfillment, and that's where you'll find your true purpose in life.

Turning Back the Clock

I'm not always politically correct. But as you might have noticed, that doesn't stop me from sharing what I see as truth.

I've been accused of single-handedly turning back the clock on women's rights, and I can see where that accusation is coming from. Joyfully serving your family? Submitting to your husband? Letting him be the head of your household?

These ideas are fading into the past as modern women would prefer to wear the proverbial pants in the family–or at least a matching pair.

I'd like to address the question on everyone's lips, "Why should husbands get the final say?" I'll start by saying this; letting him have the final say doesn't mean that you can't have a discussion and share your ideas.

A good marriage should have channels of communication by which husbands and wives both offer ideas and determine solutions. There should be mutual respect where both parties give and take of each other's thoughts. And there needs to be an attitude of acceptance where both a man and his wife can offer their voice.

But at the end of the day, he gets the executive vote. "But I would have you know, that the head of every man is Christ; and the head of the woman is the man; and the head of Christ is God."
~ 1 Corinthians 11:3.

More importantly than the obvious fact that men and women are different, the reason we submit to our husbands is because we are commanded in scripture to do so.

God's wisdom doesn't always sit right with mankind, and it doesn't have to.

Faith tells me that His wisdom exceeds mine and therefore I put my trust in His infallible Word. Yes, that's politically incorrect, and to some it may be viewed as turning back the clock on women's rights. I get that.

But really, what are the rights of a woman? Better said, what are the rights of mankind? Certainly we're given our constitutional rights, but who gives us those rights? The way I look at scripture, we're given one right and only one–the ability to choose. Anything and everything else we are given is grace.

If that's turning back the clock on women's rights, then I say turn it back and keep turning it back until men and women accept scripture as truth that is both applicable and beneficial to families today.

And if it seem evil unto you to serve the LORD, choose you this day whom ye will serve... but as for me and my house, we will serve the LORD.

Showing Up for Life -by Leane VanderPutten

The last few weeks, I have come to the realization that I am busy….very busy. I am helping with a lot of things at our parish, we have made some spiritual commitments as a family and I have become president of both the Junior and Senior Legion of Mary. I am excited about this new position because I could see the Hand of God in it, and because my family takes part in both…..but I also feel……busy.

Our Junior Legion of Mary Praesidium

Rosie makes her Legion of Mary profession at the Senior Legion of Mary.

A lot of the women I know are very busy. They have a God-given gaggle of children, many of them young. They are up night and day, doing the things that mothers lovingly….and sometimes not so lovingly (but always trying)…do.

Many of us can't change the fact that we are busy….and really, we wouldn't want to. But we must take time to smell the roses along the way….we must take the time to BE.

One of my favorite books is Achieving Peace of Heart which was written by a Jesuit priest and Catholic psychologist in a day when these could be trusted. He helped so many people and his main theme and way of recovery for small anxieties right through to mental disorders….his way of teaching the secret to happiness…was living in the present moment.

"In conscious life there is a lack of clear consciousness, or of adequate response to impressions received. A victim of this escapes from reality and from society into egocentrism. He neither lives in nor enjoys the present; he does not pay full attention to what he sees or hears. He lives in the past or the future, far away from his physical location, wrapped up in sadness, scruples, or worries….." Fr. Narciso Irala, Achieving Peace of Heart

And an excerpt from the book Hands Free Life – Rachel Macy Stafford: "Although we've been led to believe that our fondest memories are made in the grand occasions of life, in reality, they happen when we pause in the ordinary, mundane moments of a busy day. The most meaningful life experiences don't happen in the 'when,' they happen in the 'now.' This concept is not earth shattering, nor is it something you don't already know. Yet we still continually put off the best aspects of living until the conditions are right."

So….we need to consciously practice pulling ourselves back to the NOW until we become experts at it! We need to quit thinking so much of what we have to do….running, running, running. Let's do the job we are doing, let's do it well, let's think about living each moment IN the moment. This takes some effort, it takes a mindfulness that may try to elude us…. but we mustn't let it. We need to begin to show up for life.

This mindfulness will help us with our family life.

When those little…or big…. feet come running up to us and their eyes peer into ours, let's take the time to really listen and look at them. Let's BE…..for them.

So what if we are mopping the floor and want to get it done NOW! Let's put the mop aside and spend that 5 minutes listening to the latest escapade of what happened when Johnny tried to climb the tree or Susie tripped over her skip rope. Those 5 minute snatches can mean so much to them…..and to us.

(Continued on following page…)

Showing Up for Life (Con't)

When hubby comes home from work, let's take the time to stop what we are doing and greet him with a smile and a kiss. Isn't he worth it? Yes, he is worth it. If he wants to talk about his day, let's try to stay focused and listen. It won't take much of our time and it sure is a lot more important than getting those clothes off the line….we can do it later.

When 14 yr. old Jenny wants to tell us about how her book ended, or about the movie she watched (Ugh! Don't you dislike listening to someone retell a movie??), let's listen….not just listen….let's hear.

Whether we are married or single, no matter what our life occupation is, we must take time for our loved ones. This doesn't change no matter what walk of life we are in.

We want to be able to go to bed at night knowing that we have spent some time putting first things first….our husbands, our children, our siblings, our parents, our friends.

The people in our lives are so important….much more important than any chore or deadline we may think we have. We can get back to that. Let's just be there for them. Let's live in the present…..the NOW….for us, for our families.

So, for today, we will work on doing what we are doing….doing it well….and embracing those "distractions" and "interruptions" with patience and love. Let's walk with a peace, the peace of doing God's Will in the moment and not letting our mind wander too far away from the NOW. Let us BE…it's up to ME!

(Continued on following page….)

Showing Up for Life (Conclusion)

The Important Things- Leane VanderPutten
(based on "Keeping Track of Life Manifesto" – Rachel Macy Stafford)

Not the skin-deep beauty of face and figure;
Not the fullness of our bank account;
Not the speed at which I get my housework done;
Not how nice my vehicle is;
Not the cleanliness and beauty of my house;
Not the number of chores I do each day;
Not the events on my calendar;
Not the number of church functions I am involved in;
Not the text messages or emails I feel I need to respond to;
Instead....I'm paying attention to the important things in life!
I am going to live in the present, I am going to BE...
For the hugs,
For the conversations,
For the exchange of laughter to heal my anxious soul.
I am finding happiness in living for the NOW;
In the sit-down moments after meals;
In the raucous joy of children and grandchildren;
In the exchange of knowing looks that come between my husband and I.
I'm living for the NOW,
By taking the Hand of my Lord,
Looking at Him when I feel frenzied;
When I feel worried and disillusioned.
So I may be present for those I love...
my children,
my husband,
my grandchildren,
my friends.
By basking in each moment as I pause along the way,
I'm living for the NOW,
Because I know that there are more important things than accomplishing each task on my list;
Because I don't want to miss a childhood, a wedding, a friendship;
Because I want to be able to lay my head down at night knowing I have connected with those things that matter most.....
Because when my life is at its close it can be said, "You have run the race, you have fought the good fight." and I will be remembered, not for what I have accomplished, but for HAVING LOVED WELL.....

The Wife, the Dispenser of Hospitality

From True Womanhood, Rev. Bernard O'Reilly, 1893

To the wife's stewardship belongs also the discharge of a most important, not to say most sacred duty—that of hospitality. It is one of the chief functions of the divine virtue of charity.

Of its nature, its necessity, and its importance we do not wish to discourse here. Few are the homes and the hearts to which hospitality is a stranger. Those to which this book may reach will easily understand what the word means without either definition or description. We can, therefore, convey our instruction by the simplest method. Whoever is received into your home as a guest—precisely because he is your guest.....forget everything else to make his stay delightful.

It matters little whether persons thus hospitably received may or may not appreciate your generosity, your cordiality, and that true warmth of a welcome like yours, inspired by Christian motives much more than by worldly reasons; it matters much for you that none should ever enter your home without finding it a true Christian home, or should leave it without taking away with them the pleasant memory of their stay and a grateful recollection of you and yours.

Doubtless some will be found whom no courtesy, no kindness, no warmth of hospitality can change from what they are,—little-minded, narrow-hearted, selfish, cold, and unable to judge the conduct of others by any other standard than their own low thoughts and sentiments.

They are only like bats entering a banquet-hall by one window and passing out at the opposite, after having fluttered blindly about the lights, or clung for a few instants to the walls or the ceiling. Let them come and let them go. The social and spiritual atmosphere of the place is not for them.

Nor must you complain of the number. It is wonderful how much place a large-hearted woman can find for her company, even in a very small house!

A hospitable spirit can do wonders in its way: it can make the water on the board more delicious than the wines of Portugal, Spain, or France or Italy; it can make the bread which it places before stranger or friend as sweet as the food of the gods; it can multiply its own scanty stores—as the Master did with the loaves in the wilderness.

For God's blessing is with the hospitable soul to increase, to multiply, and to sweeten; to fill all who sit at her board with plenty, with joy, with thanksgiving.

"There is," says Digby, "a castle on the Loire held by a lady of ascetic piety and of noble fame, in the latest pages of French heroic annals. There one of my friends, received to hospitality, finding many guests, supposed himself surrounded by men of illustrious condition, till he was informed that they were all persons reduced to poverty, whose title to familiarity under that roof was founded precisely on their indigence and misfortunes."

Ah, noble France, how many other homes along the Loire, the Mayenne, the Sarthe, and the Somme do we not know which are always open to the stranger and the pilgrim from other lands, while their generous masters and mistresses deem every sacrifice a blessing, because performed for Christ present in the guest of one day, or one week, or one month!

"Home is where we strive to make guests feel like family, and family members feel like honored guests."
—Unknown

Hectic Days for Helen
by Leane VanderPutten

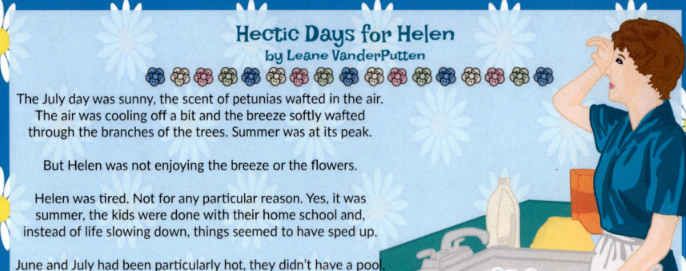

The July day was sunny, the scent of petunias wafted in the air. The air was cooling off a bit and the breeze softly wafted through the branches of the trees. Summer was at its peak.

But Helen was not enjoying the breeze or the flowers.

Helen was tired. Not for any particular reason. Yes, it was summer, the kids were done with their home school and, instead of life slowing down, things seemed to have sped up.

June and July had been particularly hot, they didn't have a pool, so the children spent time indoors during the heat of the day. Without the schedule of school, mayhem seemed to reign with more frequency than Helen liked.

Helen's husband, Mark, was working lots of hours. Summer was the time his work became very demanding because he was in the construction field. So he was not around much to help out. And when he got home he was tired and even cranky at times.

"Such is life," Helen sighed. Lately, things hadn't been working out the way she had imagined. Instead of enjoying the so-called "lazy days of summer" she was fighting inner turmoil. She was struggling through the days, battling thoughts of self-pity and complaining.

"Why can't the kids be quiet now and again?"

"Dirty diapers, dishes, it's discouraging," she thought. "And life is only going to get more and more hectic as the years go by. I just don't know if I can do this!"

This day had been particularly trying so when rosary time came around, amid the slouching children and wriggling baby, she implored Our Lady to help her.

The next day Helen woke up with a terrific pain in her side that didn't want to leave. It was debilitating so she had to call in a babysitter to take over.

That night was sleepless. The next day, after a doctor's appointment, she started an antibiotic for a bladder infection.

The antibiotic didn't work so another one was tried. That one alleviated some of the symptoms for a short while but they came back with a vengeance.

The next couple of weeks were harder than ever for Helen. The worst part was the worry. She didn't know what this mysterious pain was and, since they didn't have insurance, she wasn't going to run in and have a bunch of tests done. At least not right away.

So she was stuck worrying. What happens if it was something really bad? She'd find herself looking at her kids and imagine leaving them to fend for themselves in a crazy world.

When her husband came home, her thoughts wandered to whether he would be left alone… If this was something that could actually take her life? She pushed a lot of those thoughts away but with her melancholic nature, they kept creeping back.

After a very bad night, finally, Helen went back to the doctor….this time a different doctor. He heard all the symptoms and told her that it sounded like she was just trying to pass a kidney stone.

(Continued on the following page…)

Hectic Days for Helen (Con't)

This was news to Helen! She didn't understand why the first doctor didn't spot that?

Her step was a little lighter as she left the doctor's office even though she still had pain. She got home and drank lots and lots of lemon water and took hydrangea tincture.

Within a few of days, she passed that kidney stone and was feeling much better!

The pain was gone, but the best part was that the worry was gone! With all the imaginings of her having a dread disease she had been tied up in knots!
Now that she knew things were OK, her heart filled with joy and thanksgiving!

The following days things began to get back to normal – hectic life came back full force.

But Helen's heart had changed, indeed!

It still wasn't easy to drag herself out of bed in the morning, but her heart was filled with thanksgiving because she could actually get up and take care of her children. Were the children any quieter? No. But she appreciated the laughter and the noise instead of always fighting against it. Did hubby come home earlier? No. But she was grateful that her husband had the work that he did and was not upset that he wasn't around to help.

Her heart sang as she did the dishes.

She still got impatient, things weren't flawless, but Helen was seeing things through different eyes.

She thought back on that evening when she implored Our Lady, during the rosary, to help her. She realized how much she had helped – maybe not in the way she had wanted or expected but it didn't matter. She knew it was a gift right from her Mother's hands!

The summer days passed quickly. There were many joys in between the rough spots. Helen had learned a lesson. She hoped it would stick. She prayed it would stick.

Those weeks when things got rather dark for her taught her something special besides being grateful for the daily grind. She made up her mind that she would thank God for her crosses as she was going through them, knowing that He had the best possible plan in mind for her and that good would come from them.

It also came home to her that each new day was a gift. She would work hard at tuning her mind into that at the beginning of the day so that when the day ramped up she would have a spirit of gratefulness in spite of everything else.

As Helen sat outside in the early autumn breeze of the evening, amidst the floating aroma of the petunias, she thought to herself, "Indeed, it has been a very productive summer!"

A Wise Woman's Economy
Rev. Bernard O'Reilly, True Womanhood, 1893

We must not, especially in an age which tends daily more and more to deny that man owes any account to God for the use of the wealth he chances to possess — whether that be inherited from his ancestors, or obtained by his own thrift and industry — be carried away by the torrent of error.

No matter whence derived, all that man has as well as all that he is belongs to God — his Creator and Lord and Judge; and to Him must he return to give an account of the use which he will have made of his being, his life, his time, his property.

Reason, even without the light of supernatural revelation, teaches this truth as fundamental and unquestionable.

The great and the rich will have to account for their stewardship, —for the uses to which they have put their time, their riches, their power, their influence, their opportunities, just as the laboring poor will have to account for their thrift, and the awful uses to which one may see, day by day, our hard-working heads of families put their earnings in drunkenness, gambling, and all manner of vice.

But, as we have said, it is the province of the housewife to be at home a wise steward in the use of her husband's means, while his chief business is, outside of the home, to procure these means by honorable industry. Both are responsible to God.

The wife's immediate responsibility however is toward her husband. She is his minister, his eye, his hand, his head and heart, in applying his wealth or the produce of his industry to the ends for which God wills it to be employed.

Of persons of royal, princely, or noble rank, we do not think it necessary to treat in this place. We speak of wealth wheresoever it exists, and of the duties and responsibilities of the wife in its home-uses.

Hers should be a wise economy. Wisdom consists in a clear perception of the ends or uses for which money is to serve, and in the careful adaptation of one's means to one's expenditure.

You have so much and no more to spend each week, or each month, or each year; you have so many wants to provide for: let your wisdom be proved by always restraining your outlay so as to have a little balance left in your favor.

We know of a wife,—a young wife too,—who after her bridals was made the mistress of a luxurious home, in which her fond husband allowed her unlimited control. They were more than wealthy, and his business relations and prospects were such as to promise certain and steady increase for the future.

Still the young wife did not allow herself to be lavish or extravagant. She provided generously for the comforts of her home, for the happiness of her servants, for the duties of a generous hospitality; she had an open hand for all charities and good works.

But she was also, young as she was, mindful of the future; and this wise forethought is eminently the characteristic of women.

Without ever whispering a word of her purpose to her husband, she resolved from the beginning of their housekeeping that she would lay by in a safe bank her weekly economies.

*Continued on following page....

A Wise Woman's Economy (con't)

The husband, in all likelihood, would have deemed this saving an ill omen, pointing to future calamity. It was, however, only the prophetic instinct of the wise woman, who, in the heat of summer and the overflowing plenty of autumn, looked forward to "the cold of snow," and made store for the need and warmth and comfort of her household.

The "calamity" came after a good many years; it came by a fatal chain of circumstances in which the misfortunes or dishonesty of others brought ruin on the upright and prudent and undeserving.

One day the husband came home with heavy heart, and tried in vain to hide his care from the penetrating eyes of love. He had to break to his wife the dreadful news of their utter ruin.

She listened unmoved to his story: "All is not lost, my dear husband," she said; "I have been long preparing for this. If you will go to such a bank, you will find enough laid up there to secure us either against want or poverty."

In order to secure this wise and provident economy, even in the midst of wealth, two extremes must be avoided—parsimony, which destroys domestic comfort and makes the mistress of the proudest house despicable in the eyes of her cook, her butcher, and her grocer,—and waste or extravagance, which is ruinous to the largest fortunes and most criminal in the sight of God.

"Waste not—want not," used to be inscribed on the huge bread-platters of our fathers, both in the servants' hall and the family dining-room.

"Waste not—want not," ought to be the rule of every housewife in all departments of household economy.

Waste is always a sin against God, against your husband and children, as well as against the poor, who have a right to what is thus thrown away: and, forget it not,—waste never fails to lead to want, as surely as stripping a tree of its bark is followed by its pining away and withering.

Another rule, which a wise woman will never violate, is to tell her husband when she exceeds her means or allowance.

It is fatal concealment to allow debts to accumulate without one's husband's knowledge; it tempts the woman weak enough to do so to have recourse to most unworthy and most dangerous expedients, which are sure to be known in the end, and to lower the culprit or ruin her forever in her husband's esteem.

The equivocations and the downright falsehoods which are often used as means of concealment, cannot but be considered by every right-minded man as a greater calamity than the accumulation of the largest debt or the loss of an entire fortune.

In this respect, as indeed in every other, no concealment will be found to be the wife's only true policy; and to secure this policy of no concealment let her make it the study of her life to have nothing to conceal.

My Response is My Responsibility

Based on the Podcast My Response is My Responsibility by Emerson Eggerichs of
Love and Respect Ministries ...www.loveandrespect.com

Think about this phrase for a moment, "My response is MY responsibility". This is a very powerful phrase! There is the story of a time during WWII Nazi Regime rule. A Christian French man who had been harboring Jews had been captured. German soldiers brought him before an SS Soldier known as "The Torturer". Surprisingly to those around him, the French man was at peace and it shone through his eyes and his face. The SS officer was not impressed! Taking it as insolence, he yelled, "Get that smirk off your face!" Others who had entered into his presence were terrified and showed it.

The SS soldier once again looked at the French man and screamed, "Don't you know who I am??!!"

"Yes, I do," said the French man, "You are called 'The Torturer' and you have the power to have me tortured. You also have the power to condemn me to death." There was a pause. "But you do not have the power to get me to hate you."

This story shows so clearly the control we have to be free from sinful attitudes and responses within ourselves even under the most trying circumstances! Other people cannot control our inner world.

My Response is my Responsibility – this phrase can change our lives!

People may be able to control us physically but they cannot control our thoughts! People can treat us unkindly but they cannot control our spirit! I can rule my own inner responses – this is a God-given right. No one can make me hate them. Even the Gestapo, as worldly powerful as they seemed to be, could not rule over the French man's inner realm.

How does a person get to the point where they are no longer ruled by other's treatment of them? We begin by realizing my response is my responsibility!

We don't need to mope or pout. We don't need to give the silent treatment or let the rage build inside of us until it comes out of our mouths like a faucet – remember it is our responsibility to control our inner thoughts, those nasty habits that have gotten so out of hand. Time to look them square in the eye and say – "I don't have to listen to you....I don't have to respond this way!!"

If we let others control how we respond, then they are the master of our emotions. If they are mean and unjust, we will be unhappy. What we are saying, then, is that we are a hopeless and helpless emotional victim to the moods and attitudes of others around us! When we are around uncaring and mean-spirited people, there is no hope for us. We are at the whim of these negative people and we will have a rotten day!

This does not have to be our reality!

Are you frustrated with your husband? Do you blame him for your unhappiness? Do you say to yourself, "If he loved me properly, I would in turn respect him and all would be well?" That is making your husband "Lord" of your emotions and happiness. That kind of power should not be given to another human being.

If this is how we think, then when our husband treats us imperfectly (and he will, as he is an imperfect human being) then we are moody and grumpy; we snap at him, we let that black cloud settle over us. We resort to resentment and anger and depression. Because our husband, whom we have given power to rule over our inner spirit, lets us down, we are depressed. He is responsible for our happiness!

Ok, so let's step back..... are we saying we shouldn't be affected at all by what other people say and do? Let's take an analogy. A doctor taps our knee with a little hammer and our leg involuntarily kicks out. This is known as a "knee-jerk" reaction, right?

What about road rage? When someone cuts us off, we emotionally get angry.... but are we saying that we cannot help ourselves when we cuss at the person, try to cut him off in return or other such offensive actions? Though we have involuntary emotions, that, yes, are acceptable, there are some that cross the line....and we usually know when and what those emotions are.

If our anger is not righteous indignation, if it is unrighteous, and if it has become a habit because we have given into those emotions throughout our life, then this is wrong and needs to be turned around.

Each person tends to blame their own bitterness, harshness and contempt on the other person. We claim it is involuntary; the other person caused the anger.....

Please hear a simple and profound truth....people do not CAUSE us to be who we are, they REVEAL who we are. Ouch. My response is my responsibility. The Nazi did not cause the Frenchman to react in kindness; he revealed the kindness within him.   *Continued on following page...

My Response is My Responsibility (con't)

How many times through the day is our inner person revealed: Those times when the kids are tugging on our skirt and we snap at them "What do you want AGAIN!" Little Jill spills her milk and we look at her and say through gritted teeth, "You are the most careless child I have ever met!" Hubby comes home tired and sees no dinner being fixed and complains (maybe unjustifiably) and we yell at him and give him the silent treatment the rest of the night.

These dear ones don't CAUSE our anger, they reveal it. We do not HAVE to react this way....no, we don't. In each of these instances, we blame Johnny, Jill and our hubby. We say to ourselves, "I would never blow my stack if everyone behaved! Life stinks!"

We choose to live under the delusion that life experiences cause us to be upset and angry. Although we would never voice that we are a victim, this is how we sometimes live.

Living this way, in victim mode, changes the nursery rhyme:

"Humpty Dumpty sat on a wall,
Humpty Dumpty had a great fall.
Humpty Dumpty was pushed."

Let's just blame humanity. I would be happy if it wasn't for people! Sounds silly, doesn't it?

We have unrealistic expectations and requirements that everyone else around us (and especially hubby, since he is a grown human being) needs to meet! He must.....be perfect.

We want to assign blame; there is something inside of us that wants to justify our bad behavior.

As Emerson points out, Adam blamed Eve, Eve blamed the serpent. The serpent didn't have anyone to blame because he didn't have a leg to stand on!

Our Lord says these things come from the heart of man. It is something within us that cause us to react in these unedifying ways. I have evil thoughts because I have chosen to think bad things. I have a hateful reaction because it is in my heart. I slander because it is in my heart to bad mouth people and the list goes on....

Our response is not another's responsibility.

This message is challenging.

It is hard to face up to.

These challenges may be small, everyday things, but it can also be huge struggles and sufferings like the French man.

We do have freedom to respond with dignity.

Can I do this when my blood is boiling? Can I choose not to react angrily?

This idea of blaming someone else for my bad attitudes is inappropriate. This doesn't mean that bad behavior is to be sanctioned. This doesn't mean that the other person doesn't have to deal with their issues. They do. But that's a different matter than my response to them. This is what we are talking about here.

We must not think that if we respond with dignity and love, that we are letting the other person off the hook. We have to come to the point that we realize that we can speak what is true and NECESSARY. But we do so in a kind, loving and respectful way. This empowers us.

If we become uncorked, it does not help us to govern the situation. Your husband will eventually close his spirit if you are continually "letting him have it"! He will not want to be around you. You will have no credibility with him.

You may win a battle here and there by coming unglued and blaming everyone, but eventually you lose the war. This is a painful reality.

Let's begin to react properly. But we need to give ourselves some grace. This is a process. We may know it, but our application of it will not be perfect.

*Continued on following page...

My Response is My Responsibility (Conclusion)

Like the French man in a concentration camp who made it through….. He observed and came to these conclusions:

Our purpose as humans is not to seek power or pleasure but to seek purpose. No situation has the power to control us.

When we are no longer able to change a situation, we are challenged to change ourselves!

Everything can be taken from a man except one thing, to choose one's attitude in any given circumstance.

Between unloving or disrespectful behavior and my response, there is a space. In that space is that power to choose our response. In our response lies our growth and our freedom.

The one thing another can't take away from me is the freedom to choose how to respond to what someone does to me.

Forces beyond our control can take away everything we possess except one thing, the freedom to choose how we will respond to the situation.

Our great freedom is the freedom to choose our attitude.

The French man's story really leaves the rest of us without excuse at some level. How in the world can I come uncorked when the person cuts me off in the road, or hubby is angry?

I do have a choice. Like the French man I can change my responses.

Remember, **My Response is My Responsibility!** Will I take this to heart?

Don't Sweat the Small Stuff

Small irritations are not that important. We need to let them go. If we don't, they build up until they become a mountain that is hard to climb over.

He doesn't take out the garbage? He is always late for dinner? He is always leaving things around? He goes hunting when you would rather he stayed home? Truly, these things are not important. Overlook them and get on to looking at his better side and being thankful!

The rewards of a grateful heart are many!

-Lisa Jacobson

Marriage is a vocation; it is holy; it is a Sacrament; it is a means of going to heaven.
- Rev. Msgr. Irving A. DeBlanc

The reality of love is *unfathomable*. Could it be perhaps because it is the most **beautiful masterpiece of God?**
Fr. Raoul Plus, S.J.

"Pride must have no place in wedded life. There must never be any calculation as to whose place it is to make the apology or to yield first to the other. True love seeks not its own; it delights in being foremost in forgiving and yielding. There is no lesson that husbands and wives need more to learn, than instantly and always to seek forgiveness of each other whenever they are conscious of having in any way caused pain or committed a wrong. The pride which will never say, 'I did wrong; forgive me,' is not ready for wedded life!" -J.R. Miller

What Does Acceptance Mean?
by Leane VanderPutten

A Summary from Fascinating Womanhood:

Oftentimes in our Finer Femininity meetings we talk about "Acceptance". It is the fundamental basis for loving another.

Acceptance means that we accept our husband just as he is today, not trying to change him.

It does not mean we are blind to his faults (that doesn't happen in marriage, does it?) and it doesn't mean that he should not be a better man than he is.

It is realizing that this is his own responsibility and not our own. What a relief this! It takes a huge burden off of our shoulders!

You realize he has faults, but you realize they are just that, *faults*…human frailties.

Maybe you don't agree with his ideas, but step back and allow him his own opinion and viewpoint.

Maybe his interests and dreams seem dumb to you….or too risky. You need to allow him to follow them. That does not mean you can't discuss it with him (if you think it is important enough or if you think it will be received well), but if you see that discussing it does not change them, back off (and pray).

In accepting him, you are allowing him the right to be himself, for better or for worse.

Acceptance does not mean tolerance, that you put up with him. Nor does it mean dishonesty, that you deceive yourself into thinking he is perfect when he is not. Nor is it a matter of resignation.

Acceptance is a happy state of mind, when you realize that your responsibility is not in making him over, but in appreciating him for the man he is. Acceptance means you recognize him as a human being who, like yourself, is part virtue and part fault.

This is an honest look. You realize that his faults exist, but you focus on his virtues. You accept the total man with all of his potential goodness and all of his human frailties.

So, why don't you, today, practice accepting that man you married?

An Aura of Organization
by Emilie Barnes

The 80/20 Rule

The 80/20 rule is one of the greatest principles you can use to figure out your top priorities. If all of the items on your to-do list are arranged in order of value, 80 percent of the value comes from only 20 percent of the items. The remaining 20 percent of the value comes from 80 percent of the items. Sometimes a little more and sometimes a little less. The 80/20 rule suggests that in a list of ten projects, finishing two of them will yield 80 percent of the value.

So don't be overwhelmed by a large list. Remember the top 20 percent of the list gives 80 percent of the value. What's left undone today can go on the list for tomorrow. Rearrange your to-do list so that it is in order of priority and keep the 80/20 rule in mind.

Break It Up

To accomplish a big task, break it into a few smaller parts—these become "instant tasks" that you can easily handle. It's the big items that throw us and leave us in a panic.

Think of one project that you have put off because it seemed too big to take on after a busy day or in the middle of a hectic one.

For example, let's choose cleaning out the refrigerator as your dreaded project. Can you give it 15 minutes? Even the craziest of days usually have a few breaks in them that could be put to good use.

Set a timer and work like mad for those 15 minutes evaluating leftovers, checking expiration dates, and wiping off shelves.

Tomorrow, set the timer and toss out old vegetables, refresh the ice trays, and rinse the meat and produce bins. In a day or two you'll have invested two or three 15-minute sessions and completed the larger task of cleaning your refrigerator.

Today Is the Day!

Resolve to make each and every day count. Instead of constantly anticipating tomorrow, live for today. When you invest in tomorrow's worries or schedule, you're missing out on what is supposed to happen or be experienced today!

Have you ever spent a great deal of time fretting over a future obligation or task only to find that it was not that burdensome—but the weeks of worrying were?

Make today count toward your pursuit of a more organized life. Select one item and find an ideal place for it. Now, when that item ends up on the coffee table or on the kitchen counter, you'll know exactly where it belongs. Your quest to de-clutter your home can truly be this simple.

Get Motivated!

Your attitude is one of the most useful tools available in your desire to clean out what is cluttered and make a difference in your home or work environment. This is especially true if one of your biggest obstacles is lack of motivation.

If you look around and see a mess or a setting that doesn't suit your lifestyle, taste, or your family's growing needs, don't be discouraged. And don't let laziness or lack of motivation stop you from making a change for the better.

"Lazy people want much but get little, while the diligent are prospering" (Proverbs 13:4).

Be one of the diligent, one of the prosperous ones. Turn your negative attitude into an internal dialogue that is encouraging, supportive, and energetic. Start your day by congratulating yourself on the effort you made the day before.

Look at the cupboard you organized or the corner you finally cleared of shoes and baseball caps. Celebrate the small steps—your attitude will continue to inspire more and more effort.

A man appreciates a clean, orderly home, made comfortable and homey by the touch of a woman's hand.
—Helen Andelin

Repetition, Pattern, Order....
It is the little things in life that we do each day that will
BUILD THE MONUMENTS.

Don't bite off more than you can chew.
Do the little things......EACH DAY.
—Leane Vander Putten

A Domestic Queen is a woman who has a good attitude about her work and place in the home, and finds satisfaction in her duty. —Fascinating Womanhood

We are what we repeatedly do. **EXCELLENCE**, therefore, is not an **ACT** but a **habit**.
—Aristotle

7 Steps to Productivity
1. Go to Bed
2. Wake up at a Regular Time, Get Dressed
3. Make a List, Spiritual Duties on Top
4. Plan Your Meals
5. Keep the House Picked Up
6. Delegate
7. Don't Listen to Negative Self-Talk

—Leane Vander Putten

The Wife Desired is Patient

From The Wife Desired, Fr. Leo Kinsella, 1950's

Webster's Dictionary has this to say about patience. Patience is "uncomplaining endurance of wrongs or misfortunes." Patience "denotes self-possession, especially under suffering or provocation." It also suggests "quiet waiting for what is expected" or persistence in what has been begun. Forbearance, leniency, and sufferance are given as synonyms.

Patience is a quality of maturity. Little children are not noted for "uncomplaining endurance of wrongs." Mother would begin looking for the thermometer should she notice anything resembling "quiet waiting for what is expected." It takes a bit of living and dodging of the "slings and arrows of outrageous fortune," before people get enough sense to value patience.

Patience connotes a "self-possession, especially under suffering or provocation," and it brings to one a quiet confidence. The patient wife is master of her own soul. She, and not every imp to come flying into her mind, is in charge of her own fort.

Since no one can be truly successful without patience, it should be expected that the possession of the virtue is a requisite for every desired wife.

Indeed, no vocation or profession in life requires patience more than that of husband and wife.

The first reason for this is that they live in such proximity to each other. They rub elbows day in and day out. There is bound to be a little chafing here and there. Among saints there would be. Patience is the soothing oil preventing the irritations from becoming running sores.

Some years ago I was faced with the necessity of working up a talk on the ideal wife. Naturally, I was open for suggestions, particularly from a few ideal wives whose friendship I highly prize.

One evening, as I visited the home of one of these friends, I mentioned the task with which I was confronted.

"Mary, if you had to give an hour talk on the ideal wife to high school seniors or to a woman's club, what would you discuss?"

Here was the voice of experience talking. I was not asking any air scout how to fly that Constellation. The senior pilot of the airlines was briefing me now. I was not asking any campfire girl how to whip up that batter of soda biscuit mix. Grandma herself was looking over her glasses at me.

I think that it is of interest to point out here that, although she did not indicate that she considered patience the most important quality of the desired wife, she unhesitatingly suggested it first.

Not only did she mention patience first, but she also explained what she meant by patience in the wife.

Notice that the discussion deals with the patience required of the wife, not of the mother in her relations with her children.

A woman is first the wife of her husband before she is the mother of his children. Later I hope to say a few words concerning the twofold role which the woman must play.

At present I just want to make it clear that Mary is no rattle-brain. She was on the ball and stayed there. She was explaining what she meant by the patience in the wife and her dealings with her husband.

Marriage is not a fifty-fifty proposition. (This of course, is Mary talking through my memory.) The wife who enters marriage with the misconception that it is, has failure lurking just around the corner. Often she will think that she is giving her fifty percent. As a matter of fact, it is only fifteen or twenty percent. On many other occasions the husband unconsciously is demanding ninety percent. The fifty percent proffered falls miserably short. The result is two people at loggerheads. A fight begins and love takes a beating, if it is not turned out-of-doors.

(Continued on following page...)

The Wife Desired is Patient (con't)

The understanding, the sympathy, and the patience required for happy living cannot be measured out. The stupid expression "marriage is a fifty-fifty deal" implies yardsticks, tape measures, half cups, full tablespoons, and the like.

Love has nothing to do with these things – will not be fenced in by them, for love partakes of the very limitlessness of God.

A wife's parsimonious measuring out of her imagined fifty percent produces many serious fights. She wins these fights and loses her husband.

Let us illustrate the above by concrete examples.

The wife was getting supper ready. John was fighting the traffic on his way home from work. She was humming softly as she busied herself contentedly about the kitchen. He was muttering loudly the "red light blues". She felt fine. He was half sick and out of sorts. Things had not been going well at work. He was upset and unwittingly looking for a fight.

As he entered the house and gave Mary a little hug and kiss, she noticed that he looked tense and jumpy. A few minutes later she could hear him scolding one of the children. The storm warnings should have been flying by now. They had better steer clear of him tonight.

Before the family was called to the supper table, Mary had been fully on guard. Unless she was very mistaken her husband was going to demand much more than fifty percent somewhere along the evening. So the measuring devices, the half-cups and full tablespoons were behind her for this evening.

The meal was already prepared. She would not use them on her husband. She would not measure out her patience and understanding. Her husband was definitely off-color this evening. She would give him her all. No matter what he said, she would pass it off.

The supper got off to as good a start as could have been expected with the cloud hanging over the table. Soon one of the children massacred table etiquette in such manner as to cause Emily Post to wince.

Before her husband could draw in sufficient breath to let out a blast at the culprit, she quickly took the wind out of his sail by firmly correcting the child. Before the dessert appeared, she took in her stride a caustic remark about the quality of the pot roast and a criticism leveled at her through one of her children.

Mary was nobody's dish rag. She had a lot of fire and spirit. She could have stood up to him that night, "let him have it," and have had a fight which she might have won, or, at least in which she would have held her own. But, did anyone ever win a fight of this kind?

This ideal wife had made up her mind to carry her husband through the evening, come what might. He was not himself.

Tomorrow would be another day. If he had been physically sick in bed and needed her care, would she have given only fifty percent? Of course not. She would have nursed and lavished upon him all the warmth of her nature.

Well, he was sick that night – sick in mind and spirit. He needed her intelligent, loving and patient consideration. She would have considered herself a very shallow person to have reacted otherwise. She was in love with her husband that night too, unreasonable though he was.

A few weeks later the tables were turned. She was the one who was at wits end with herself. She started the day with a headache and things went from bad to worse. It was a rainy day, and for some unfathomable reason the school shut its doors on the children.

They were under her feet all day. Often she had to act as referee in their squabbles. As the afternoon wore on toward supper time, she was becoming conditioned for more adult opposition.
(Continued on following page....)

The Wife Desired is Patient (con't)

An unsuspecting husband made his entry. He was back to his little castle in the suburb with roses round the door (metaphorically speaking) and babies on the floor (literally speaking).

During the meal Mary "blew her top" about something. Oh yes, the car did not start that afternoon. The battery or something must have been dead. Some junk! It was time they had a new car.

So it was a junk, was it? John could think of the days of work it had taken to buy that old bus a few years previous. It was still a good car. What did women know about cars anyway? There ought to have been a law against women ever—-.

There is no future in this kind of thought, so John quickly banished the hideous little devil from his mind. Mary was worked up tonight. He would have to be cautious. Did he defend his car against his wife? John was a little too sharp for that.

He jumped on the band wagon and lambasted the car too. Yes. We would have to do something about that nuisance. He felt like going out then and burning it up. He knew that by the time they got to the dishes, she would have forgotten all about the car.

Mary purred through the rest of the meal contentedly with that wonderful feeling that her husband was all for her. Together they stood against the whole world.

Suppose that John had been a little thick between the ears and that he took exceptions to her remarks about the car and defended the car against his wife. A fight would have ensued. Feelings would have been hurt. And there was danger that their tempers would have swept them on to the name calling stage. Once this has been reached, real harm frequently has been done to a marriage.

Mary finished her explanation of what she meant by patience by saying that she and her husband had never had a fight in the twelve years of married life. Then she added what I thought was the epitome of her whole conversation by saying that she and her husband did not intend to have any fights.

This determination not to fight was indicative of their intelligence and maturity. Surely it was one of the factors contributing to the happy stability of their marriage.

This couple has had arguments and disagreements, I believe that I have been in on a few warm ones. An argument is not a fight.

People with minds of their own will not always see eye to eye on every phase of their daily lives. Viewpoints will vary and disagreements will result even as to whether or not junior should have a crew haircut. But let us not make junior a ward of the divorce court because husband and wife cannot agree on the proper length of junior's hair. After all, it is not that important.

Arguments and disagreements degenerate into fights, when ill-feeling, name-calling and bitterness come into the picture. The ideal wife, fortified with the virtue of patience, sets her face against such loss of harmony. Whatever be the cost she wisely realizes that her effort at peace is worth the price.

No good comes from fights in married life. I have been asked whether it is not a good idea for husband and wife to have a fight once in a while. The air is thus cleared. The very young, theorizing about this, often add that it is so sweet when they make up. In connection with this question one inquirer quoted Bishop Fulton Sheen as saying that a couple never really knows how much they love each other until they have made up after their first fight.

Nothing was said about how many found out how little they loved each other and never made up. It is very true that sometimes good comes out of evil. Yet, how insane it is to seek or even permit avoidable evil, on the chance some good might come of it.

Fights among married people are evil things and bring untold misery into lives. So many broken marriages have come before me in which there was no third party, no drinking, no in-law trouble, no major difficulty. They just fought. So often people are less mature than their children, whom they have brought into the world to endure their bad tempers.

Fights begin between human beings because of pride. We have a will of our own. When we do not get our way pride suffers. Like children we want to fight the opposition to our will. So far we have no control of our reactions. We are made this way.

(Continued on the following page....)

The Wife Desired is Patient
(Conclusion)

♥♥♥♥♥♥♥♥♥♥♥♥♥♥♥♥♥♥♥♥♥

If we are adults, however, we have learned by bitter experience that our pride is the surest destroyer of happiness and love. Unless we are psycho-masochists, we crush our insurgent pride and prevent ourselves the stupid and dubious pleasure of hurting the one who has stung our pride.

Once a fight has begun between man and wife it is clear that one or the other must win the struggle against pride. One or the other must curb the desire to win the empty victory.

If the wife makes the first effort at reconciliation, her humility will make it difficult for the husband to nurse his pride. Pride cannot face up to humility. It is shamed out of existence.

Even when husband and wife make up completely after a fight, a fight is still unfortunate. Fights leave scars. The wound heals, but there ever remains a scar in the mind.

I have had many estranged married people tell me that their partners did this or that to them twenty-five or thirty years ago. Happy years had intervened between the fight and the present estrangement. But they could not forget, even if they had forgiven.

The wife desired meditates deeply on the hatefulness of fighting. She has made up her mind to suffer anything rather than fight and thus wound her husband. Remember that there is always the danger that we begin to hate whom we hurt for the same reason that we begin to love whom we help.

Our Thoughts....Our Destruction or Our Salvation

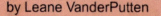

by Leane VanderPutten

There is a saying, no not just a saying...a Bible verse. I'm sure you have heard it. Here it is from the Douay-Rheims Bible:
"But the things which proceed out of the mouth, come forth from the heart, and those things defile a man."

What it says is that those things that come from the mouth, the things that we speak, have already been in the heart before we speak them.

In our relationships, especially with our husband, we have to be very careful of the thoughts that we allow to fester within our minds, and therefore in our hearts.

It starts with little thoughts....a little self-pity here, a little indignation and bitterness there.

"He didn't pay any attention to how I was struggling with taking the garbage out....what an un-chivalrous man I married!" Boom! That one is on the bottom of the Thought Pile for the day.

"There he goes again...harping about what isn't done instead of seeing what is....what a jerk!" Boom! Pile it on top of the last one!

"Why doesn't he clean up after himself....so lazy!"
"He doesn't ever ask me how MY day was....he is so self-centered!"

Wow! The pile is getting bigger, isn't it? On and on it goes... And these thoughts could be in a span of a half a day....or half an hour! Can you imagine a whole day of thoughts like this?!

These thoughts will come, we cannot control our feelings and life is what it is. People have faults and you married a man that is imperfect.

These are temptations. What we do with these temptations is the important thing....the very vital thing. These very thoughts, that start off so small, can either lead us on a destructive path or a path of joy and freedom.

You say these thoughts are insignificant. Let's look at an example...

You take an alcoholic who has suffered much because of his alcoholism. He has quit drinking and is experiencing a life that he never thought possible. He is gaining respect from those around him, his family is supporting and encouraging him and life is good once again after many long years of pain.

Why would this man ever turn back to drink when he compares the two roads...the horrific one he was on or the path he is on now? It couldn't be possible that he would go back to drink...but...it happens all the time.

Do you know why? Because of a thought....a thought that he did not nip in the bud and cast out before it had begun to branch out its little tentacles, ready to strangle him when he was weak.

This happens with all the sins....sins of impurity, anger, gluttony, etc.

*Continued on following page...

Thoughts (Con't)

So these thoughts, these bitter and resentful thoughts you coddle in your mind, are not insignificant. I believe that once you open the door to these kind of "little" cracks and crevices, the foundation to your most important relationship in life begins to become weak and one day, when you have given in and given in to disrespecting your husband this way, the devil will come along, feed you a line, and you will cause damage that may be irreparable.

We MUST overcome and change these thought processes no matter how hard it may be and how long we have been giving in to them. It is God's will for our life. He wants us to love, to be kind, and, as a wife, to respect our husband and the position he holds in our lives.

We will let God do His work on our husband…. That is not our business…we know what work we have to do. And He will most certainly bless us for it.

We must be on guard against our own negative thought patterns and work to overcome them. They are not little things, they can turn into monsters.

Just as the alcoholic would give up his whole new life because of a thought, so negative, self-pitying, bitter thoughts are a slippery slope that could eventually ruin a perfectly good marriage.

We need to realize the seriousness of this and stay on top of it….by reading good books, hanging out with positive people, listening to good podcasts, praying, going to daily Mass, etc.

What if we are really struggling in our life? We may feel overwhelmed and tired….meals to make, children to tend to, husband to keep happy, etc., etc.

We may feel we cannot do it anymore…we can't overcome, it is too exhausting! And we are right. On our own, we cannot.

Let's remember to turn to Our Lord and rely on His grace to overcome. All the helps that we, as Catholics, have…the Masses, the Rosary, our Sacramentals, the Sacraments…will help us stack up graces so we can continue the good fight. It is very worth it!

We have about 40,000 different thoughts going on in our heads each day. What do they consist of? Do you just let your mind have free reign? How's that working for you?

What do YOU think of each day?
We do not want to give in to mental laziness! If we try we can always turn our thought processes around.

But that is the clincher. We must recognize when our thoughts are going down a bad road and then we must make the effort to change them.

Remember, what our hearts hold inside will spill forth in our words. Are these words going to work toward our destruction…or our salvation? It is up to us. It is simple, but not always easy.

God never gives us more than we can bear so roll up your sleeves and do what it takes to turn your thoughts around…to a brighter, more positive outlook!

Home Warming
by Emilie Barnes

Surrounded by Beauty

Beauty is as necessary to the spirit as food and clothing are to the body. Fortunately, beauty is easy to invite into any home, for beauty has many faces. Beauty can be found in a hand-colored photograph or a hand-stitched quilt, or in shelves lined with bright-hued jelly jars. A pot of graceful ivy can be beautiful and so can a sweet potato vine growing in a jar.

Even the arrangement of a home can be beautiful. When furniture and objects, whatever the cost or the style, are combined with care and attention, the result can be warmly beautiful, even if the individual pieces are less than lovely.

What is beautiful to you? What makes you smile or your spirit soar? That is the beauty that should surround you in your home, and it will be shared with all who come to visit.

Seek out beauty in whatever form it speaks to you. Surround yourself with beauty. In the process, you will be creating something truly beautiful as well: a lovely home graced with a happy, welcoming spirit.

Personal Touches

I feel immediately at home in houses where people have surrounded themselves with what they love. I like to walk into a house and immediately have a sense of what they read, what they collect, what they like to cook, how they like spend their time. (This gives me something to talk about as well.) I enjoy meeting well-behaved pets and seeing evidence that there are children in the home.

Our home overflows with objects that remind me of who I am and what I love. Clusters of family photos – on a wall of our great room, on a table in the bedroom, on my desk, and on the refrigerator – fill the spaces of our home with smiling, familiar faces.

Teacups from my long-time collection retell their stories to me each time I look at them. My mother's secretary and my auntie's crystal build a bridge for my memories. Books and signs and plaques collected on our trips fit together like pieces that make up the puzzle of our lives.

Somehow, it all manages to come together in a homey atmosphere that says, "This is who we are. This is what we love. Please have a seat and let us get to know you, too."

Cleanliness Creates Hominess

Bob used to tease me that I would die with a broom in my hand. And it's true that the first thing I usually want to do when I come home from a trip is grab a broom and sweep off the front step. I love that sense of getting my home in order. To me, it's hard to feel comfortable and at home in a house that is dirty, cluttered, or disorganized.

Create a comfortable nest where people you love, including yourself, can work and play and relax and visit without worrying about whether they will step on a toy or be faced with a discouraging pile of undone chores.

It Takes a Lifetime

It takes a lifetime, this process of making yourself a home.

Homes grow and change just as people do. But these simple secrets of "at-homeness" hold steady through the ongoing homemaking process.

Make yourself comfortable – and create a comfortable environment for yourself and others.

Add the little touches that make a house feel like a home.

Surround yourself with beauty.

Surround yourself with you.

Create peace by ordering your environment.

Above all else, listen to your dreams of home. Allow them to guide you as you learn to make yourself and others happily at home.

Quotes

Fix him his favorite meal and your best dessert, put on some soft romantic music, give yourself enough time to look your best, and you're all set for when he gets home. He'll feel like a king and know he's a top priority in your life! -Emilie Barnes

Happiness in marriage must be earned. It is something you must work out for yourself, chiefly by forgetting yourself and serving others. No marriage is a success unless you make it so, and that takes persistent effort and, still more, a constant and humble reliance on God. – Fr. Lawrence G. Lovasik

Every effort we make to forget self, to leave self behind us, and to devote ourselves to the labor of making every person with whom we are bound to live, happy, is rewarded by interior satisfaction and joy. The supreme effort of goodness is,—not alone to do good to others; that is its first and lower effect,— but to make others good. -Rev. Bernard O'Reilly

At any rate, she has by nature the power, the art, and the disposition to please, to soothe, to charm, and to captivate. It is a wonderful power; and we see daily women exerting it in a wonderful way. Why will not women who are truly good, or who sincerely strive to be so, not make it the chief study of their lives to find out and acquire the sovereign art of making their influence as healthful, as cheering, as blissful as the sunlight and the warmth are to their homes? – Rev Bernard O'Reilly, True Womanhood, 1894

As a family, try to lead a hidden life with Jesus in the Holy Eucharist. Through holy Mass, offer yourselves through Mary's hands as a sacrifice with Jesus; at Holy Communion, you will be changed into Jesus by divine grace so that you may live His life; by your visits to the tabernacle, you will enjoy His friendship in the midst of the many problems of life. -Fr. Lawrence G. Lovasik (Photo from our daughter's wedding)

Honor his position as the head of the family and teach your children to do so. Have faith in the principle that God placed him at the head and commanded you to obey him, as stated in the Bible. If this doesn't seem fair, remember that God's ways are better than our ways.
Helen Andelin, Fascinating Womanhood

A man feels 'successful' when he knows his woman is behind him – no matter what his other accomplishments may be. He needs to know that she believes in him...That she thinks he's a terrific husband (not perfect – just terrific). A first-rate guy. And, if there are children, that he's a fine dad too....That she thinks the world of him, even though he might mess up or make mistakes. – Lisa Jacobson

Lord, Help me to be a good wife. I fully realize that I don't have what it takes to be one without Your help. Take my selfishness, impatience, and irritability and turn them into kindness, long-suffering, and the willingness to bear all things. Take my old emotional habits, mindsets, automatic reactions, rude assumptions, and self-protective stance, and make me patient, kind, good, faithful, gentle, and self-controlled. Take the hardness of my heart and break down the walls with Your battering ram of revelation. Give me a new heart and work in me Your love, peace, and joy. I am not able to rise above who I am at this moment. Only You can transform me.
-The Power of a Praying Wife

Unloving.....Disrespectful

Based on the **Love and Respect** Book by Emerson Eggerichs

Does it seem to you that often the interactions with your hubby, when you are supposed to be "communicating", can end up in frustration and hurt?

Do you say something with good intentions only to be misinterpreted by him, an argument starts, feelings are hurt and you wonder how in the heck that just happened?

This month, in our Finer Femininity meeting, we talked about what Emerson calls the "Crazy Cycle". Remember, in my article "Who Is Right?" (page 8) we talked about a man and a woman having different opinions, preferences or tastes and how they end up in conflicts because of this. We found out that neither of them is wrong, they are just different. This last meeting we saw what happens when something is misinterpreted as disrespectful to the husband, and he in turn says something that is unloving, so she returns it with disrespect and he answers unlovingly....etc., etc. Round and round it goes, maybe day after day and year after year. This is called the "Crazy Cycle".

Emerson gives an example:

Their first Christmas as newlyweds, his wife sews him a very nice jean jacket. She spends hours and hours on it. Christmas morning she saves this best gift for last and hands it to him with expectant excitement.

He opens it, takes it out and looks at her, smiles and says, "A jean jacket! Thank you!"

That was it.

She's a little deflated. She asks him if he really likes it.... he says he does. She needles him and asks him again if he truly does like it and he answers that he does. Then she says that it seems he doesn't like it and he reassures her that he sincerely does.

She doesn't believe him.....

You see, in her family, when someone was given a special gift, the thanks were profuse and long-lasting. It was ooooed and ahhhed over. It was brought up again and again.

This was what she was used to, so she misread her husband's reaction. She began to get what seemed like disrespectful to him.

He interpreted her interrogation as questioning his integrity so he started to get irritated and came off as being unloving. She couldn't believe it! After all she had done for him (the jacket), he would treat her this way! And so her disrespect rises, which in turn brings out more unloving remarks from him....etc. etc. Round and round it goes.....

THIS is called the CRAZY CYCLE and these little misunderstandings can turn into hurt feelings, resentment and building walls. And they can last for years and get bigger and bigger.

Ladies, who is going to jump off this merry-go-round first? Well, since we are mature women who want to heal our relationship.....we are!!

We have to stand back and ask ourselves, Am I coming off as disrespectful?

We must understand that a man needs respect....and this is his vulnerability. No, he is not narcissistic, neither does he have a big ego. That doesn't mean he isn't sometimes selfish and egotistical (he is not a perfect man)...but in general he is a good-willed man and respect is very important to him.

So....when you are having a conflict with him, or even just a conversation, watch your words and your tone.

(Continued on the following page....)

Unloving.... Disrespectful (Con't)

Emerson says:
"If your husband has good will, you have power to affect him through your unconditional respect. When your husband feels disrespected, his spirit may deflate. What does that mean? More than likely, it is the critical point right before his behavior changes to what appears unloving (he stonewalls or he becomes harsh, sarcastic, or angry). When this happens, challenge yourself to take note of what you just said or did. Take responsibility for your part and see what happens. If though, you hold onto your disrespect as his fault, and refuse to confess and make adjustments, you deprive yourself of this influence."

Remember, we expect our hubbies to love us unconditionally, even if we are at times not very lovable. In turn, we should give to him unconditional respect even if he doesn't always deserve it. Lastly, Emerson asks us to practice having a "quiet spirit". Our husbands will be won by a respectful behavior and a quiet spirit (1Peter3).

"This is central to your empowerment as a wife. This is not sexist teaching. Just as your husband needs to learn to live with his wife in an understanding way, which touches her spirit (1Peter3:7), you need to learn the discipline of a quiet spirit which opens his heart."

5 Ways to Love your Husband
1. Tell him that you love him and what you love about him
2. Pray for him - often
3. Respect him
4. Be kind and compassionate
5. Be affectionate with him

The Time-Warp Wife

"The best thing that you can do for your marriage is to pray for your spouse every day."
— Darlene Schacht

"When I count my blessings, I count you twice."

"If you want your husband to trust you with his heart as he once did, it's important to practice self-control, hold your tongue, and replace criticism with kindness. Listen when he talks and make an effort to show him respect." -Darlene Schacht

"The truth is, the less you communicate your complaints, negative thoughts, and criticisms to your husband, the better your intimacy will be, and the stronger your marriage." – Laura Doyle

Financial Distress? There Is an Answer....

The Infant of Prague is called the Patron of Financial Distress. Yes He is…and He helps in so many other ways, too!
After 30 years of here and there wishing for a lovely statue of the Infant of Prague, hubby ran across one at an estate sale! Imagine that! And with all the colorful gowns and 2 crowns! What a find!

It is not the statue, of course, that makes this devotion possible. It is our heart's devotion, the prayers we say to Him…AND He does especially help with finances! Who, in their married life, doesn't need help with finances at some time or other?

Here He is watching over things for the summer on top of our covered wood stove. I had Him dressed in red for the Precious Blood since it is July but halfway through I changed him to this lovely peachish orange…a summery color! I go to Him for many things and when there is an urgent need (and I find that those come up often in a big family) I will do the 9 hour Infant of Prague Emergency Novena.

I am including that novena at the end of this article. We have so much amazing help at our fingertips….POWERFUL help! And that is why I am sharing this with you….we all need help. And many times, it can be financial…which is a true stress!
So….turn to the Infant of Prague in your needs. And if you can find a small statue somewhere (we have a smaller, very nice one that was given to us by a friend and that we use also… pictured on the bottom), spend the money on it, get it blessed and put it in a place of honor. He will take care of you!

Quote: "The more you honor me the more I shall bless you."

The Infant of Prague is invoked against financial distress. His statue has a crown because He is the King of the world. His right Hand is raised in blessing and the globe shows He holds the entire world in His hand.
Honoring the Infant of Prague is a tradition that is kept in many homes throughout the world as He is believed to guarantee financial stability and abundance. There are several novenas to the Infant of Prague. One reflects the intensity of an emergency situation, and is to be done in one day's time, the prayer said once every hour for nine consecutive hours.
Devotion to Christ as a young Child dressed as a King has its roots in the Carmelite Order of Spain. According to tradition, in 1555, Saint Teresa of Avila gave a statue of the Christ Child, dressed in actual royal robes to a noblewoman who was marrying into an aristocratic family in Bohemia.
Taking it with her to what is now the city of Prague, her daughter, the Princess Polysenia inherited it. In 1623, Princess Polysenia was widowed and chose to devote the rest of her life to charitable causes.
*Continued on following page….

Financial Distress...There is an Answer (Continued)

When she saw the need that the poverty-stricken Carmelite order had, she donated the statue to them, saying, "I give you my dearest possession. As long as you venerate this Image, you will not lack anything."

The monks credited this image with the immediate upturn of their fortunes. When they were forced out of their monastery due to a war in 1631, they left the statue behind and the invading army threw it in a rubbish heap. Within seven years the Carmelites were back in their monastery in Prague, desperately attempting to rebuild it. One monk, Father Cyril, who had a particularly strong devotion to the Divine Infant found the little wax statue among the rubble. The only damage done to the statue was its crushed hands.

It was decided that the scarce funds the community had should go to more practical things than the repair of a statue. As the monks struggled to rebuild their former home and church, Father Cyril heard the words: "Have pity on me and I will have pity on you. Give me my hands and I shall give you peace."

After the statue was repaired, the monks again displayed it in the main church. As the city of Prague suffered an epidemic, parishioners began invoking the little statue for aid. The quick answer to their prayers brought many in the surrounding region to seek help.

Gradually, the devotion spread to many other countries.

Today, the church in Prague built to hold the statue, Our Lady of Victory, is a site of pilgrimage with visitors from all over the world paying their respects to the Divine Infant.

Infant of Prague Church
(Our Lady of Victory)

Infant of Prague Statue

Nine Hour Devotion to the Infant of Prague

O Jesus, Who has said, ask and you shall receive, seek and you shall find, knock and it shall be opened to you, through the intercession of Mary, Your Most Holy Mother, I knock, I seek, I ask that my prayer be granted.
(Make your request)

O Jesus, Who has said, all that you ask of the Father in My Name, He will grant you through the intercession of Mary, Your Most Holy Mother, I humbly and urgently ask Your Father in Your Name that my prayer be granted.
(Make your request)

O Jesus, Who has said, "Heaven and earth shall pass away but My word shall not pass", through the intercession of Mary, Your Most Holy Mother, I feel confident that my prayer will be granted.
(Make your request)

Nine Day Novena to the Infant of Prague

O Infant Jesus, I run to You, begging You through Your Holy Mother to save me in this need (you may name it here), for I truly and firmly believe that Your Divinity can defend me. Full of trust, I hope in You to obtain Your holy grace. I love You with all my heart, I am painfully sorry for my sins and on my knees I beg You, O Little Jesus, to free me from them.

My resolution is to improve and never more to offend You. Therefore, I offer myself to You, ready to suffer everything for You and to serve You faithfully. I will love my neighbour as myself from my heart for the love of You.

O Little Jesus, I adore You, O Mighty Child, I implore You, save me in this need (you can mention it here), that I may enjoy You eternally, with Mary and Joseph and with all the angels. Amen.

9 Ways to Nurture Your Love

100 Ways To Love Your Husband by Lisa Jacobson

1. Make his dreams...your dreams. Treasure them like your own. Ask him about what he hopes to do some day and let him know that you believe in his dreams...and him. Plan out together the steps you can take to make those dreams come true.

2. Be extravagant in your love. Go big. Pour out your heart generously.

3. Feeling edgy? Snappish? Droopy? It tends to come with the territory – just avoid taking it out on him. It's not really his fault, after all. Speak his love language – what says love to him. And speak it often!

4. Ask him the kinds of things that make him feel loved by you. He might have an answer ready and he might not. If not, then ask if he'll think about it.

Also, you can study him and watch for those things that seem to fill him up and make sure you're saying it to him. Don't make accusations. Ask questions.

5. Intertwine your lives wherever possible. Run errands, go for walks, curl up on the couch. Just seek to be together. Don't wait for "date night" to find things you share in common.

6. Forgive. "A happy marriage is the union of two good forgivers." ~ Ruth Bell Graham. This is one of the truest statements ever made. Decide you're not only going to be his lover – you're going to be his forgiver. Be quick to forgive and get good at it. You'll probably have lots of opportunity to practice it.

7. Then forget. Once it's been forgiven, put it behind you and never pick it back up again. Here's the hard part: letting it go. Resist the temptation to grab it back and maybe even throw it at him when it happens again. I'm sorry, but this doesn't count as true forgiveness. Forgive as God has forgiven you— as far as the east is from the west (Ps. 103: 12).

8. Cling to each other in the hard times. Don't let trials pull you apart, but be sure they bring you closer together instead. This decision is best made before the trial comes.

9. Start each day with a smile and a kiss. What better way to begin? Set the tone for the day with a simple gesture of love for each other.

Always Choose Love

From 100 Ways to Love Your Husband by Lisa Jacobson

Celebrate your Anniversary

Do something special together and recognize the grand occasion that it is. It doesn't have to be fancy or expensive, just thoughtful and memorable. Do the same thing each year. Or maybe your tradition can be to do something different each year.

Don't hang out with friends who put him – or their own husbands – down.

So destructive. Let your friends know that you love them, but that you are incredibly loyal when it comes to your man. You won't stand for put-downs or critical remarks. If they love you? They'll want to support you and your marriage.

Tell him how attracted you are to him.

Let him know about the magnetic pull you feel for him.

Back him up in his decision-making.

He'll value your support. As much as possible, go with his lead. This will give him confidence and, most likely, make it that much easier – if or when – you do disagree with him. He'll be more likely to listen to and respect you because he knows you wouldn't go against it without good reason.

The Lord can heal your hurts.

Your husband cannot. So don't resent him for something he can't do. Psalm 147: 3

Write little love notes.

Tuck them in his lunch. Or write on the bathroom mirror. Send a text or a quick email. Passing secret love notes never goes out of style.

Embrace your differences.

If you were both the same? How boring would that be. So rather than trying to form him into a male version of yourself, be glad you each have your own unique strengths and personality.

Express enthusiasm for his plans and ideas.

Worry about the practical application and serious possibilities later. Let your first response be positive and encouraging! That's what gives him courage to try new things and consider new adventures.

Keep tenderness in your love.

Don't let hardness or sharpness creep in to make it brittle. Protect your love from outside pressures and stresses that can spill over into your relationship with him.

 Always choose love – again and again.

About the Author

Mrs. Leane VanderPutten lives in rural Kansas with her husband, Vincent, of over 30 years. She is the mother and grandmother of 11 children and 28 grandchildren and growing.... They are devoted to Tradition within the Fold of the Catholic Church, homeschoolers, with 4 children still at home. Their family life is lively.... full of faith and joy!

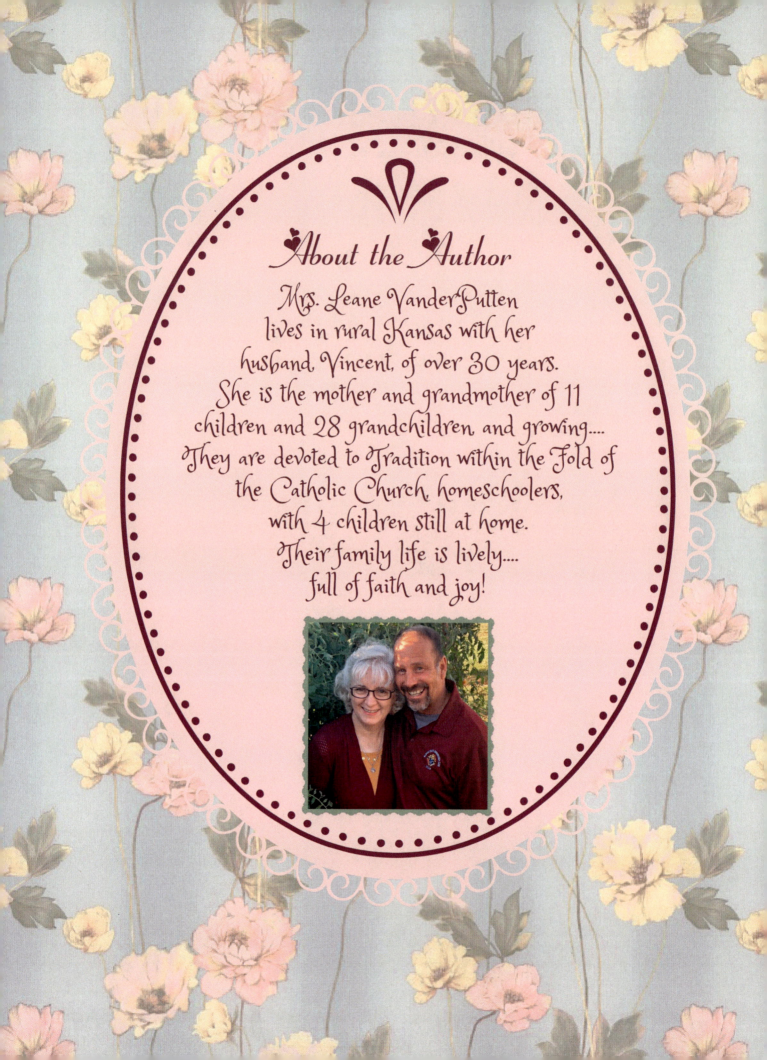